# Create Wealth By Preserving Capital

# Create Wealth By Preserving Capital

Mark W. Eicker

Copyright © 2016 Mark W. Eicker
All rights reserved.

ISBN: 1539495035
ISBN 13: 9781539495031
Library of Congress Control Number: 2016917136
CreateSpace Independent Publishing Platform
North Charleston, South Carolina

# Testimonials

"Investors of all experience levels will gain insight into the power of rules-based strategies to avoid good portions of bear markets by reading this book."
Kenneth Kim, PhD
Chief Financial Strategist, EQIS

"*Create Wealth by Preserving Capital* offers investors unique approaches to be better prepared for the next market downturn."
Jerry Minton, PhD
President, Alpha Investment Strategies

# Table of Contents

Testimonials · · · · · · · · · · · · · · · · · · · · · · · · · · · v
Book Foreword · · · · · · · · · · · · · · · · · · · · · · · · · ix
Preface · · · · · · · · · · · · · · · · · · · · · · · · · · · · · · · · xi
Acknowledgments · · · · · · · · · · · · · · · · · · · · · · xiii
Introduction · · · · · · · · · · · · · · · · · · · · · · · · · · · xv

Chapter 1   The Early Years · · · · · · · · · · · · · · · · · · · · · 1
Chapter 2   Business Plans on Cocktail Napkins · · · · · · · · · · 9
Chapter 3   Why Asset Allocation Doesn't Work as
                 Well as High Conviction · · · · · · · · · · · · · · · · 16
Chapter 4   Reinterpreting Asset Allocation · · · · · · · · · · · · 29
Chapter 5   Disco, Oil Embargo, and Gold:
                 The Wild 1970s · · · · · · · · · · · · · · · · · · · · · · 39
Chapter 6   Behavioral Economics Theory · · · · · · · · · · · · · 49
Chapter 7   The Evolution of Rotation Theory · · · · · · · · · · 57
Chapter 8   Preserving Wealth · · · · · · · · · · · · · · · · · · · · · 64

                 Bibliography · · · · · · · · · · · · · · · · · · · · · · · · · · 71
                 Author Bio · · · · · · · · · · · · · · · · · · · · · · · · · · · 73

# Book Foreword

THIS BOOK IS a must read for anyone worried about the devastation that bear markets can wreak on investment portfolios. It begins with the euphoric 1990s investment environment and the lessons learned along the way. I now have a better understanding behind the authors' desire to create lasting strategies that tackle various factors that could impede wealth generation. You will learn some simple strategies that can be used to perform well during both bull and bear markets. Readers will also become familiar with some of the most common mistakes that investors make.

Tom Lydon
Editor and Publisher, ETF Trends

# Preface

THIS BOOK CAME to fruition after more than twenty years of managing investor assets. This is a story about making mistakes and learning from those mistakes. It describes the journey that three young men began together in the early 1990s and that culminated in the creation and management of Sterling Global Strategies. More importantly, it details simple investment methodologies that can be put to use, allowing anyone to potentially create wealth by preserving capital.

# Acknowledgments

MY BUSINESS PARTNERS, Mike Haig and Greg Carroll, and I began working together back in the early 1990s. We've been through many good times and some bad ones. We essentially grew up together, experiencing weddings and children's births and a few funerals along the way. On September 11, 2001, we sat together around a single bubble-butt television and watched in horror as the second plane flew into the World Trade Center. That was a somber day for every American, and we watched it together for the next couple of hours. For those of you who remember, the entire country basically shut down that day. I can vividly picture the three of us having lunch at Marie Calendar's and discussing what had happened. That is but one memory of thousands over the past twenty-three years. I thank Mike and Greg not only for their partnership but also for their support and friendship.

To our research analyst, John Nance, thank you for the high energy you bring into the office every day. You deserve a lot of credit for this book being written. Thank you for all your help editing and helping me when writer's block set in.

My parents, Walter and Mary, passed away many years before they should have. They instilled in me at an early age the qualities that make me who I am today, and I thank them for their unconditional love and support.

To my sister, Kim; brother-in-law, Joe; nephews, Joey and Johnathon; and niece, Lauren, thank you all. You've always been there for me, and I couldn't have received a better gift in life than to have you as my small but wonderful family. Kim is seven years my elder and has always taken a parental role in my life, especially after our father passed. I appreciate how much you care more than you will ever know. Thank you all very much.

To my in-laws, Willy and Josephine, thank you for accepting me into your family. It is wonderful to be able to call the two of you Mom and Dad.

To my lovely wife, Rozlyn, you have supported and loved me through thick and thin. You are not only my wife but my best friend, my confidante, and my partner. We have already experienced so much together. We have many more chapters of our lives to be written, and I wouldn't want to live them with anyone but you.

# Introduction

PATRICK HENRY WAS correct when he said the only way to judge the future was to look to the past. He was speaking about governance, but the quote covers many aspects of life, including investing. As of this writing, low interest rates are potentially causing bubbles to develop in the equity, bond, and real estate markets. Bubbles have taken place throughout history, and valuable lessons can be learned from each. The last bubble to burst was the real estate bubble in 2008. The most famous of all the bubbles and generally described as the very first one was the tulip bubble of 1637.

At the peak in March 1637, a single tulip bulb sold for ten times the annual income of a skilled craftsman. At one point, as described in the Charles Mackay book *Extraordinary Delusions and the Madness of Crowds*, a single tulip bulb was traded for twelve acres of land.

The popularity of the tulip is thought to have begun in 1593 in what is now the Netherlands, after a Flemish botanist perfected a tulip bulb that could tolerate the harsh conditions of the area. The tulip had an intense petal color that was coveted and unlike any other plant of the time. During this period, Amsterdam was at the center of the lucrative East Indies trade route and was minting many citizens' fortunes. Many of these folks, not unlike those today, chose to flaunt their newfound wealth by building grand estates, and the tulip was considered a status symbol that they all demanded in their palatial gardens.

With so much money chasing the tulip, prices went up for decades as demand increased far faster than supply. The bulb that was the most sought after suffered from the mosaic virus, which produced a color-breaking pattern. Producing these bulbs took many years, and historians now believe the number of bulbs that feverishly changed hands during the later years of the tulip mania may have been roughly the same number that it began with.

In 1636 a type of futures market was created on which contracts could be bought to purchase the next year's crop. This market was informal, transactions were between individuals rather than through the exchange, and for the most part, no tulips were actually changing hands. Prices skyrocketed due to ever-increasing numbers of people entering the tulip market through futures contracts who never intended to own the bulbs. The bubble began to burst in March 1637, when buyers of tulips declined to show for bulb auctions, immediately driving the inflated prices down. There is speculation that this may have occurred due to an outbreak of the bubonic plague. In any case, the tulip bulb made many people fortunes that were only to be lost overnight.

## Create Wealth By Preserving Capital

Disciplined investors who understand how to use technical analysis have the tools to avoid the majority of bubble collapses. Remaining disciplined is extremely difficult during periods of underperformance but is usually rewarded in the end. Understanding that every investing strategy has an Achilles' heel and knowing what that shortcoming is can help investors remain disciplined in their methodology.

CHAPTER 1

# The Early Years

*Be fearful when others are greedy and greedy when others are fearful.*

—Warren Buffett

Along with Michael Haig and Greg Carroll, my partners at Sterling Global Strategies, I began my investment career in the early 1990s at Shearson Lehman Hutton, which after many name iterations eventually became Smith Barney and today is Morgan Stanley.

We were young and energetic and, in those early years, trying to figure out which group of investors our practice would specialize in. We decided we wanted to focus our energy on companies in Southern California, setting up and servicing retirement plans. We were told by many advisors in our office that this was a foolish plan. They told us how many had failed pursuing the 401(k) market before us and had washed out of the business. Instead of heeding their advice, however, we persevered, and through blood, sweat, and a few tears along the way, we were advising many companies on their retirement plans. So many in fact that we were asked to join the 401(k) advisory group at Smith Barney in 1996, which at the time consisted of fewer than one hundred employees. This put us on the map at Smith Barney and helped us make the leap to providing more comprehensive corporate services to both private and public companies.

In 1997 we officially formed a corporate-services team in San Diego and worked closely with the investment bankers out of New York. It proved to be a cozy little relationship. The investment bankers would point out companies that they wanted to form a relationship with, and we would make introductions to the executives of those firms. These were typically companies that were used to working with third-tier investment banks and were itching to be clients of the venerable Smith Barney. These were also companies that Smith Barney would have never looked at, save for the fact that these were the go-go 1990s, and share prices of many local technology stocks were doubling and then doubling again. The executives, however, were not aware that they were already on our investment bank's radar.

At meetings we would point out the obvious to the frothily anxious executives, who would have signed a contract with the devil if it would have procured the services of Smith Barney's investment bankers: the easiest way to have access was to begin producing revenue for the firm through our corporate-services team. As I mentioned, there was a cozy little relationship between our team and the bankers. In hindsight, perhaps it was

## Create Wealth By Preserving Capital

a tad bit deceptive, but it was nevertheless highly effective. We were young, and we had been told this was how business was done.

Our pitches to the executives of these public companies, outlining the benefits of Smith Barney's capabilities regarding stock option and stock purchase plans, cash management services, and pension and 401(k) asset management, were all but formalities. These executives wanted access to the Smith Barney investment bank's capabilities, and they saw us as the way to get it.

One such public company was headquartered in San Diego. Let's refer to them as the AAA Corporation. AAA was producing semiconductor chips for the burgeoning computer and telecommunications sectors. Everything from computers and laptops to cell phones and scanners uses semiconductors to send information electronically. Every year, the size of the chips was decreasing while their speed was doubling. Computers were becoming obsolete every couple of years. At the same time, everyone in the developed world was buying either a new computer or their very first one. Technology companies were growing rapidly. It mattered not if the line of business was producing cell phones, computers, or scanners; creating online commerce or Internet connectivity; or supplying semiconductors for integrated circuits. The space was booming, and the tide was raising each and every one of these companies' stock valuations.

Young investment enthusiasts reading this book will be amazed at the stratospheric trajectory of this stock. Between

## Mark W. Eicker

January 1998 and October 2000, AAA skyrocketed from $9.56 per share to more than $400.00 per share, split adjusted. Because of the stock option plan that was in place, the receptionist at the front desk became a millionaire—at least on paper. Happily for her, she did not let greed become part of her psyche as she began to unload stock options beginning in the $250.00-per-share range and retired a millionaire. Others were not as fortunate.

By the mid-1990s, stock option plans had become all the rage within the technology sector as a way for companies to obtain and retain the best talent in the world. Options were handed out to newly hired employees as an inducement to choose ABC Company over XYZ Firm and offered to employees of XYZ to induce them to leave and join ABC. The option contracts gave the owners the right to buy the stock at a predetermined strike price. There was typically a two-year vesting period during which the employee could not sell the stock, which locked them into the company for that period of time. If an employee left prior to his or her option contracts vesting, the options would be forfeited. Within most companies, all employees would be given additional option contracts every six months, which were also vested over a two-year period.

At AAA most of the early employees had option contracts with strike prices as low as $1.00 per share. As time went by, the option strike prices varied wildly as the stock launched higher. Why is the strike price so important? The strike price allows the option holder to buy shares of the underlying stock at the strike price. If the stock is trading at $100.00 per share

## Create Wealth By Preserving Capital

and the option holder controls one thousand option contracts with a strike price of $1.00, he or she would pay $1,000.00 for one thousand shares of stock valued at $100,000.00. Most companies, AAA included, allowed their employees to perform this whole function without changing the option into stock. The employee would simply exercise his or her option contract and in this scenario receive a check for $99,000.00.

Our recommendation to every employee and executive of AAA who would listen was to sell enough of the stock to invest in tax-free bonds that would pay an income stream equal to their current pay so they would be able to retire with the lifestyle they had grown accustomed to. For some that was as little as a couple million dollars, and for others the number was in the tens of millions of dollars. Still, in most cases, the values of the stock options the employees owned were many multiples higher. Some of the employees would sell a small lot of options and regret it the next day as the stock price of AAA continued to surge, and many refused to sell more or wouldn't sell a single option contract to begin with.

In those days all anyone could talk about within the walls of AAA was the value of the stock and how much everyone was raking in. Who could blame them? Most of the top executives owned millions of option contracts with strike prices (the price they had to pay to exercise the right to own the stock outright or to sell) in the low single digits. Take, for instance, an executive who owned a million option contracts with a strike price of $2.00 a share. When the stock was trading at $10.00 a share, they owned $800,000.00 in option equity; at $400.00 a share, the value of the option contract was nearly $400,000,000.00. These were pretty heady days for the employees at AAA.

At some point during 1999, we began to notice an influx of Porsches, Ferraris, and such in the parking spaces that were once occupied by Toyotas and Ford pickup trucks. The employees who were selling small numbers of stock options were obviously more concerned with luxury items than retirement. Most folks we spoke to had bought into the argument that the equity markets had entered into a new paradigm, driven by technology and the computer; with it came the idea that the equity markets would continue to move higher indefinitely. If this was your belief, why in the world would you sell any of it? Greed had overtaken nearly all of them.

There were some who heeded our advice to sell at least enough option contracts to be able to retire comfortably, and most of them remain clients to this very day. Others followed our advice to sell a certain percentage of their option contracts on a monthly basis and continued to do so, even after the stock hit $400.00 and began to fall from the October 2000 highs. These were the fortunate ones.

During the early days of 2000, you could feel the euphoria and excitement when walking through the large foyer and through the wooden office door that led to one of AAA's production facilities, which was lined with offices on the outside. The large room had always been bustling, but now the energy had taken on the almost magical quality that happens when so many people become filthy rich and work closely together. By now most of the employees had grown tired of our stale

## Create Wealth By Preserving Capital

soapbox pitch to protect themselves for if or when the stock reversed. AAA had recently passed the $300.00-per-share mark and seemed destined to continue higher. The room seemed to become quieter and lost some of that magic as more and more employees noticed we had entered the room. The more passionate we became that they should protect themselves and their futures by selling some of their options, the less we were trusted inside those hallowed walls.

AAA hit $400.00 in October of 2000 and then began to fall, as the tech bubble was popping. As the stock was rising, we would tell employees that the stock could retreat back to $50.00 per share, and we continued to echo those comments as the stock was falling. Many employees thought we were crazy, and some probably thought we were heretics for saying such a nasty thing about their one and only stock. A few others heeded our advice as the stock was falling and sold enough to maintain their lifestyles in retirement. One of those employees ended up retiring in Idaho on a large ranch, spending his days hunting and fishing.

The fall from grace was just as fast as the rise from nothingness. The stock fell below $200.00 during November 2000, then under $100.00 during March 2001, and below $30.00 during September 2001, wiping out more than a billion dollars of net worth within the company. The once-euphoric atmosphere had become almost somber. Fear had set in, and the employees were worried the stock would head lower. And it did. By September 2002 the stock had slid almost back to where it began, falling below $12.00 per share.

These executives and employees had learned a rare but valuable lesson about fear and greed. It's a balancing act, and being emotional while investing in their case wiped out fortunes. This is an extreme example during an unprecedented era, but watching this event unfold before our eyes was the catalyst for testing the Sterling tactical rotation strategy.

We were interested in figuring out how to avoid asset classes that were experiencing prolonged bear markets and to stay invested in asset classes entrenched in long-term bull markets. During periods when all asset classes were falling in unison, we wanted to have the ability to utilize cash as a security net. Much of this occurred because of the lessons we learned working closely with AAA.

There are many other examples of fear and greed, emotions that have destroyed lives since the beginning of time. Investors across the world were buying technology stocks during the late 1990s, and many folks had their holdings allocated much more aggressively than their risk tolerance would allow. Far too many investors waited to sell at the exact wrong time, when they simply couldn't take the losses anymore. Many never returned to the equity markets. Those who did repeated their mistakes during late 2008 and early 2009, and many of them never returned to the equity markets. Had these investors focused more on risk-adjusted returns than on top-line growth, they might have stayed invested and profited during the bull markets of 2009 through 2016. Instead, greed made them allocate too aggressively, and then fear caused them to sell deep into bear markets.

CHAPTER 2

# Business Plans on Cocktail Napkins

*Human beings have demonstrated talent for self-deception when their emotions are stirred.*

—CARL SAGAN

DURING THE LATE 1990s, nearly all technology stocks were soaring higher. The technology-friendly NASDAQ composite rose 85.6 percent during 1999. Qualcomm alone was up by more than 1,400 percent during the year. Any IPO or equity with *dot com* in its name took off like a rocket ship. I don't remember the name of one company, but it produced paintballs, and when it went public, it named itself *Blank.com*, and the stock soared. There were stories of companies filing for IPOs following nights out drinking with business plans written on cocktail napkins. More companies than we can mention had little or no revenue and were losing money but still minting their founders' fortunes. The term *the new paradigm* was introduced and suggested that the computer and the World Wide Web would revolutionize the globe to the point at which bear markets would never happen again. This lured the masses into the equity markets at a frenzied pace.

There was a segment on CNBC that captured the mood of society during the late 1990s. During the segment a blindfolded monkey threw darts at a wall on which stock tickers were written. Every ticker the monkey hit with a dart was put into its portfolio. The network then pitted her portfolio against a professional portfolio manager's best equity ideas. Sure enough, the monkey was consistently beating the professionals.

This was during a period when investment clubs were all the rage. Typically, a group of friends would meet at someone's house and discuss the equity markets and which stocks the group would buy. Some groups would pool members' assets together in the same discount brokerage account, and others would invest individually but own the same equities. There was an air among many of these groups that bordered on cockiness.

One such group based in San Diego was run by the husband of one of our personal clients whom we had met through a doctor pension plan. She trusted us, but her husband could not understand why our performance was so much worse than that of his investment club. "My San Diego–chapter investment club is destroying you," he would say. I remember the words clear as day. That's how many times I had to listen to his rants about our team's inferiority to his superior investment club. We would explain the merits of a well-diversified portfolio and that growth equities in general were priced historically high, but he would have none of it. We would take out charts of the S&P 500 dating back to 1926, which also showed average price/earnings ratios for every year on record to highlight how expensive equities had become. He would point out that times had changed, and there was absolutely no reason that the technology revolution would ever end. It did end, however, and crashing down with it was the notion that investment clubs would become viable alternatives to advisers and professional asset managers. In the end, controlling risk is much more important than sizable returns to the upside.

The technology-heavy NASDAQ composite fell more than 80 percent during the bear market that began the next decade. It took fifteen years and a 500 percent return for the index to get back to breakeven. Alternatively, a moderately invested asset-allocation model that fell 20 percent during the bear market only needed a 25 percent return to get back to breakeven. There's the difference. All the hard work that our team and advisers across the country put in to keep clients on the right path was rewarded, and we all made a difference for so many families' lives and futures.

The roaring bull market of the 1990s and the proliferation of discount brokerage firms brought day traders to the forefront of this investment world. Tens of thousands of people left their well-paid, corporate-America jobs to become day traders. These folks would trade intraday, looking to profit by buying high and selling higher. While they operated using different strategies, the common denominator was that they were all trading technology stocks, and they were raking in huge profits.

We had only one client who day-traded, and it was through a fee-only portal at Smith Barney that allowed her to trade without commissions. She set up the account sometime during 1997 with $100,000.00, which represented a small percentage of the family's assets. She provided us a firsthand glimpse into the world of day traders.

In the beginning she would occasionally ask our advice on stocks that she wanted to buy before she placed her orders. She was calling us a half dozen times per day. While we gave her our opinions, we quickly realized she wasn't following them. Our fundamental values did not match her strike-it-rich mentality. Companies like General Electric and McDonald's weren't moving fast enough. She abandoned all high-quality positions for overpriced technology stocks such as Cisco Systems, Dell Computer, Qualcomm, and any other name that was flying higher. She punched out buys and sells at what seemed to be record speed, and she was loving every minute of it. She was telling everyone she knew about the success she was experiencing and preaching to them to get involved in this money grab.

The office and computer that she and her husband once shared was remodeled with a large mahogany desk and four brand-new Dell computers, which gave her access to information more quickly and easily. Her husband often joked that he had given her $100,000.00 so she would have something to do and he would have some time to himself. If that were true, it worked. She became obsessed with the exhilaration she felt,

## Create Wealth By Preserving Capital

seated behind her shiny new toys making trades and making money.

Reading financial statements and dissecting cash flow and earnings were not part of her investment methodology. She didn't look at charts or worry about how extended a stock was on a technical basis. This left all stocks at her disposal, even those with little or no revenue that were losing money hand over fist. She didn't get caught up in the minutiae of learning what a company did, nor did she care. She had very little knowledge of technology in general. Companies to her were ticker symbols, nothing more and nothing less.

What she looked for were stocks that were making big moves higher. If they continued to move up, she would hold them, and if they started to move lower, she would sell. Buy high and sell higher was her theme, and it worked marvelously. Her early success turned her hobby into an obsession. She took great pride in her new profession, telling everyone that her occupation was day trader. In her mind she was one of the great stock pickers of the day. She compared herself to the S&P 500 and was beating it handsomely. She simply could not understand why anyone would own the boring companies (ticker symbols) that made up the majority of the S&P 500 index.

While her haphazard investment methodology would not work during most investment cycles, during the go-go late 1990s, she was killing it. Her initial $100,000.00 investment was soon over $500,000.00, and by this time her husband was singing her praises as well. She continued to trade the tickers that were flying higher, and her portfolio would eventually swell to more than $1,200,000.00. We tried as hard as we could to rein her in, but she was having way too much fun. There was no stopping her now. She thought that one day books might be written about the prowess she exhibited by typing in ticker symbols with ease. The death-defying courage she exemplified when executing trades. How a woman with no investing experience made a fortune in the stock market. She was the best of the best, she surmised. After all, she was beating almost all the mutual fund managers at the time.

What she failed to acknowledge, whether out of naivety or convenience, was that nearly all technology stocks were racing higher and that even blindfolded monkeys could perform well in that type of environment. She continued to trade through the beginning stages of the bear market. We persistently attempted to get her to see the value of old, stodgy companies and even (yikes) bonds. These conversations always fell on deaf ears.

By the time she had traded her account back down under $100,000.00, someone from Smith Barney in New York became involved and also had conversations with her. She would tell this person that she would no longer trade the account, and that might last a day or two. Then she started up again. Smith Barney eventually closed down her account when she had depleted it to below $50,000.00, under the pretense that they could not allow her to commit financial suicide.

Hers is a cautionary tale of believing that short-term success will translate over long periods of time. It also speaks of how excitement, obsession, and the thrill of the trade can eventually lead to disaster. Like a heroin addict chasing her first high, she too was chasing the high she experienced while raking in profits all the way back down.

Having her as a client taught us a valuable lesson that we continue to employ today. Attempt to stay fully invested while equity markets are rising, and run for the hills or rotate into other asset classes when equities begin to fall.

Legendary hedge fund manager George Soros often talks about reflexivity. Once an asset class begins to rise, it often continues to move higher. Conversely, when it begins to fall, the asset class usually continues lower. Had our client been a student of the market and learned the tenets of investing from the most successful investors of all time, she might have fared better. Luckily, she and her husband are still wealthy and living in a very affluent neighborhood in San Diego. She was one of the fortunate day traders of the era.

CHAPTER 3

# Why Asset Allocation Doesn't Work as Well as High Conviction

> Wide diversification is only required when investors do not understand what they are doing.
>
> —WARREN BUFFETT

THE IDEA OF asset allocation in the investment world began to flourish during the 1990s, following the Nobel Prize for Economic Sciences being awarded to Dr. Harry Markowitz for his seminal paper on the theory of financial economics. While it created a stir within the academic community, it took nearly forty years for the investment world to adopt these ideas, which were first outlined in Markowitz's 1952 paper. The bestowment of the Nobel Prize on Markowitz in 1990 validated his concepts within the financial industry, and asset-allocation models took their first major step toward popularity.

## Create Wealth By Preserving Capital

The young Harry Markowitz wrote the paper while attending the University of Chicago. He had spent some time contemplating a topic for his dissertation and decided he would apply mathematical theories to the equity markets. Most of the academic literature at the time focused on maximizing the value of portfolios through stock selection. It occurred to him that owning a single security, if it were the correct one, would maximize the value of a portfolio. However, he also realized owning a single security was extremely risky and, therefore, not prudent. He wanted to understand how one could control risk within a portfolio by using mathematical theories. Utilizing that framework, he settled in on variance as a way to measure risk by recognizing that portfolio variance depended on the covariance of securities.

"Somebody asked me, did I realize that I was going to get a Nobel Prize for that, and I said no, but I knew I was going to get a dissertation; I would get a PhD." His dissertation paper, "Portfolio Selection," was first published by *The Journal of Finance* in 1952. Simply put, it used complex mathematical formulas to determine which asset classes could be combined to optimize performance with the least amount of risk. In the paper he debunked the widely held belief that diversifying with enough securities would eliminate risk. He found that the only possible way to completely eliminate risk would be to create portfolios comprised of *negatively correlated asset classes*, but a portfolio like that would also have zero return. For instance, a portfolio that included two asset classes that always moved in lockstep in opposite directions would have zero risk and zero return.

Dr. Markowitz has been credited as the pioneer of asset allocation. He says, "Somehow my contribution was not diversification. It was a theory that took into account correlations." He understood that owning a highly diversified portfolio of perfectly correlated securities would not reduce risk at all. Instead, one needed to build portfolios taking into account the variance of assets to the covariance of other assets, which today is what we describe as correlations.

By investing in a number of low-correlated asset classes and adjusting the percentages allocated to each, an investor could optimize the expected returns of a portfolio for each increment of risk. This was essentially the theory behind Markowitz's "efficient frontier" hypothesis. A conservative investor could adjust the percentage of assets within a portfolio to include fewer stocks and more bonds, for instance. Theoretically, this would lower the expected risk of the overall portfolio but also lower the return. In contrast, an aggressive investor could do the opposite and raise the expected return and, with it, risk. The efficient frontier was the optimal expected return for each increment of risk, thereby allowing practitioners to adjust the portfolio for individual risk tolerance.

In other words, if an investor wanted to annualize 8 percent over a period of time, Markowitz's formula was designed to combine low-correlated assets in the percentages that historically would have annualized 8 percent with the least amount of volatility or risk. In contrast, if an investor's risk tolerance could only accept a 10 percent decline in his or her portfolio, Dr. Markowitz's formula was designed to construct an allocation that historically would not lose more than 10 percent but spew out the highest rate of return for that level of risk.

As mentioned earlier, few investors were implementing the concept of modern portfolio theory that Dr. Markowitz pioneered prior to 1990. The floodgates opened soon after he won the Nobel Prize. Computing power had progressed to a point that allocations along the efficient frontier could be tested effortlessly, and at the same time, major brokerage firms were searching for solutions that would ultimately commoditize their advisers. These brokerage firms believed their advisers were spending too much time managing assets and not enough time raising them. More assets meant more profits added to the bottom line, and they saw asset allocation as their golden goose. It was also viewed as a way to mitigate litigation from disgruntled clients. How could anyone sue for losses when the process they were selling won a Nobel Prize? Asset allocation was the panacea that brokerage firms across the country began to implement, and they continue to do so today.

Asset allocation is predicated on the idea that no one has the ability to predict when asset classes will enter into bear markets. If investors can't make this prediction, it is essential to put together portfolios that include assets with very low correlations. Some assets will be in bear markets while others are in bull markets, and by owning all of them, an investor can expect to be somewhere in the middle. Below is a periodic table that shows the premise behind asset allocation over the past sixteen years. As you can see, asset classes overperform and underperform during different economic cycles.

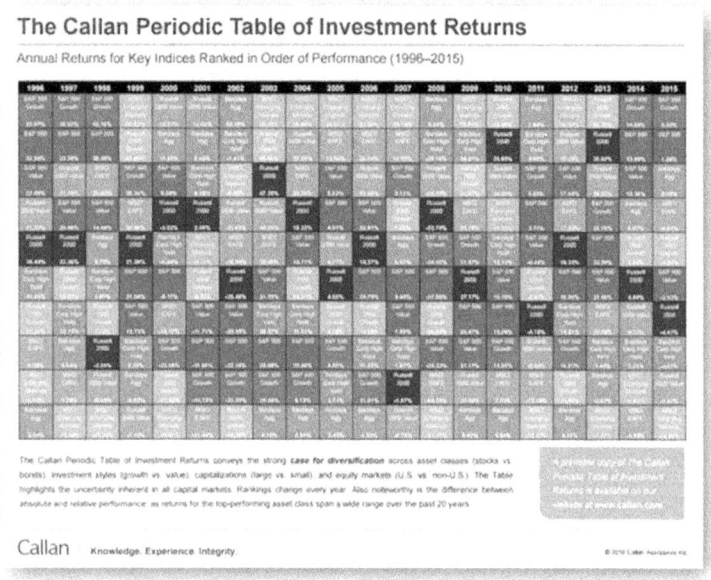

First published in 1999, the Callan periodic table of investment returns is patterned after Mendeleev's periodic table of the elements and shows returns for nine asset classes, ranked from best to worst. Each asset class is color coded for easy tracking.

The periodic table is used to sell investors on the idea of asset allocation. It is used during almost all presentations and is highly effective because it explains the concept without showing actual performance. The fact is a 60/40 portfolio doesn't keep up when the markets are rising and can still lose significantly during bear markets. The Morningstar

## Create Wealth By Preserving Capital

Balanced Exchange-Traded Fund (ETF) Asset Allocation Portfolio for instance was down 24.14 percent during 2008, while S&P 500 lost 37 percent. Morningstar was then up only 9.75 percent during 2013, trailing the S&P 500 by more than 20 percent.

We at Sterling Global Strategies believe that using relative strength and moving averages can produce portfolios that avoid asset classes in bear markets, therefore reducing downside risk while outperforming over full market cycles. The idea that no one can predict when an asset class is entering into a bear market has always puzzled us. Bear markets in US equities last on average around twelve months, commodity bear markets around seven years, and US-bond bear markets for eighteen years or so. One need not avoid an entire bear market to reduce risk and increase performance; avoiding some or most of bear markets is sufficient to help risk-adjusted returns.

An example of how to avoid asset classes in bear markets is by using a very rudimentary seven-month price change factor (MPC) for the S&P 500. We at Sterling do not use the seven-month relative price change for determining our allocations (nor would we disclose our proprietary formulas), but it serves as a basic example of just how easy it is to avoid most of a US-equity bear market. To compute the seven-month price change model, we will look at the adjusted closing price of the SPDR S&P 500 ETF (SPY) on the last trading day of every month and compare it to the closing price seven months prior. If the price of SPY is higher than it was seven months ago, buy or hold SPY, and if the price is lower, sell or remain in cash. The analysis does not account for money-market dividends during the periods the strategy would have been in cash. This strategy is either 100 percent invested in SPY or 100 percent invested in a money-market account. Below is a chart showing the performance of the S&P 500 from December 31, 2000, to December 31, 2015, versus the performance of the simple seven-month price change factor.

| Year | SPY | 7 MPC |
|---|---|---|
| 2015 | 1.23% | -4.26% |
| 2014 | 13.46% | 13.46% |
| 2013 | 32.30% | 32.30% |
| 2012 | 16.00% | 16.00% |
| 2011 | 1.91% | -1.91% |
| 2010 | 15.07% | 3.51% |
| 2009 | 26.36% | 22.43% |
| 2008 | -36.80% | 0.00% |
| 2007 | 5.14% | 5.14% |
| 2006 | 15.84% | 15.84% |
| 2005 | 4.82% | 4.82% |
| 2004 | 10.69% | 8.18% |
| 2003 | 28.19% | 22.56% |
| 2002 | -21.58% | -13.29% |
| 2001 | -11.76% | 0.00% |
| 2000 | -9.74% | -7.07% |
| $100,000 | $186,000 | $282,000 |

The data for this simple factor performed well during both bear markets. The seven-month price change model would have been down 19.42 percent during the bear market from 2000 through 2002 versus a 37.54 percent decline for SPY. During the 2008 bear market, the seven-MPC model broke even, while the S&P 500 fell 36.80 percent. Through the

## Create Wealth By Preserving Capital

entire sixteen-year period, $100,000.00 grew to $282,000.00 using the seven-MPC model, while SPY grew to $186,000.00.

On top of that, downside risk was mitigated as well. The largest calendar-year loss for the seven-MPC model was 13.29 percent, and for SPY, the largest calendar-year drawdown was 36.8 percent. Keep in mind this test was done over a short period of time and, therefore, the formula may not perform well during other market conditions or periods of time.

Also realize that turnover is high in this style of investing, and taxes will be a drag on performance in nonqualified accounts. However, this serves as a great example of how simple factors can be used to avoid part or most of bear markets.

Now let's take a look to see if the same formula will work for international equities. For the benchmark and to compute our seven-MPC model we are using the iShares MSCI EAFE (EFA) from the period spanning December 31, 2002, through December 31, 2015, and the Brandes International Equity mutual fund (BIIEX) from December 31, 1999, through December 31, 2002. EFA's track record does not go far enough back to calculate, and we wanted to provide the same length of data for our international equity exposure that we showed for equity exposure in the United States. Again, we are not including money-market returns in this example for the periods we are invested 100 percent to cash, which would have increased returns during most of the 2000s. The chart below shows how the seven-MPC model would have compared to the international equity benchmark.

| Year | EFA/BIIEX | 7 MPC |
|---|---|---|
| 2015 | -0.98% | -8.31% |
| 2014 | -6.19% | -2.10% |
| 2013 | 21.44% | 21.44% |
| 2012 | 18.76% | 10.95% |
| 2011 | -12.21% | -6.19% |
| 2010 | 8.16% | -8.72% |
| 2009 | 27.00% | 20.06% |
| 2008 | -41.03% | 0.00% |
| 2007 | 9.95% | 9.95% |
| 2006 | 25.81% | 25.81% |
| 2005 | 13.31% | 13.31% |
| 2004 | 18.95% | 14.95% |
| 2003 | 40.32% | 39.17% |
| 2002 | -19.84% | -5.09% |
| 2001 | -19.66% | 0.00% |
| 2000 | -17.06% | -17.06% |
| $100,000 | $133,000 | $245,000 |

This test produced results similar to those in our US equity simulation during bear markets. The seven-MPC model lost 21.27 percent during the 2000 through 2002 bear market, while the Brandes International Equity fund fell 46.57 percent during the same period. In 2008 the seven-MPC model had broken even, while EFA collapsed, losing 41.03 percent. Over the entire sixteen-year simulation, $100,000.00 would have grown to $245,000.00 in the seven-MPC model and to only $133,000.00 using our benchmark. This is the compounding effect of avoiding most or all bear markets.

## Create Wealth By Preserving Capital

Downside exposure on a calendar-year basis was also muted for the seven-MPC model, with the worst performance being in the year 2000, when it fell 17.06 percent. The benchmark, on the other hand, experienced four years of losses, as bad as or worse than those of the seven-MPC model, with the largest quarterly calendar-year drawdown of 41.03 percent.

Now that we have looked at the domestic and foreign equity markets, let's see how the simple seven-MPC formula performs with a bond allocation. The bond market has been in a prolonged bull market since 1981, when ten-year Treasury bonds topped out with yields above 17 percent. As of this writing, they are trading below 2 percent. As yields drop, bond prices increase. Conversely, when interest rates rise, bond prices decrease. This simulation occurs during the second half of the current bond bull market. One would hope that the formula would allow an investor to capture most of the upside without being whipsawed in and out of positions. If that were the case, one could assume that, in a prolonged bond bear market, the formula would also allow an investor to avoid most of the losses while sitting in a money-market account with a yield that's increasing along with interest rates.

In this simulation we will be using the Pimco Total Return Bond Fund (PTTRX) as the benchmark and also the instrument we are rotating in and out of using the seven-MPC model. The chart below shows the results.

| Year | PTTRX | 7 MPC |
|---|---|---|
| 2015 | 0.75% | -0.48% |
| 2014 | 4.71% | 3.32% |
| 2013 | -1.90% | -3.01% |
| 2012 | 10.37% | 10.37% |
| 2011 | 4.19% | 2.41% |
| 2010 | 8.58% | 8.58% |
| 2009 | 13.88% | 13.88% |
| 2008 | 4.90% | 4.44% |
| 2007 | 9.11% | 7.81% |
| 2006 | 4.08% | 3.50% |
| 2005 | 2.83% | 2.83% |
| 2004 | 5.15% | 5.15% |
| 2003 | 5.59% | 5.59% |
| 2002 | 10.16% | 10.16% |
| 2001 | 9.55% | 9.55% |
| 2000 | 12.20% | 12.20% |
| $100,000 | $270,993 | $250,001 |

The results were as expected. The rotations created a minor drag on the seven-MPC performance over the full simulation, trailing by $21,000.00. However, with interest rates historically low, the drag on performance over the full period could be looked at as insurance for a bond bear market. When this begins is anyone's guess; however, bear markets always follow bull markets, and as we discussed earlier, the average length of a bond bear market is eighteen years.

The seven-MPC model did not make a rotation until March 2006 and did not rotate during nine of the sixteen years of the simulation. In total, there were nine buys and nine sells out of a total of 192 months, keeping turnover at a manageable rate.

Most folks under the age of seventy-five have never invested through a bond bear market. These markets can be nearly as devastating to a portfolio as equity bear markets. A rule of thumb for figuring out the downside risk of a bond ETF or mutual fund is to look at the duration of the portfolio. If the portfolio has a duration of eight years, simply change the duration into a percentage, that is, 8 percent in this scenario. For every 1 percent rise in interest rates, the portfolio should expect to lose the percentage of its duration. Should interest rates rise 1 percent, the portfolio example above should expect to lose roughly 8 percent. A 2 percent rise in interest rates would result in an expected loss of 16 percent and so on. And everyone says that bonds are safe?

This may be one of the worst periods in history to be an investor in general, especially as a retiree. Equity and bond prices are at historic highs, and with them comes elevated risk for losses. Over the past thirty-five years, bonds have provided investors a cushion for their portfolios during equity bear markets. That is unlikely to happen over the next decade or so. In addition, the search for yield has made many investors buy instruments outside their risk profile, opening them up for the possibility of devastating consequences.

We attempted to give examples for a simple formula designed to debunk the notion that no one can predict when asset classes enter a bear market, and therefore, utilizing asset allocation is the only way to reduce overall risk in a portfolio. In the next chapter, we will take a look at how this process can be implemented in a real portfolio and see how it performs against a typical 60/40 portfolio.

Many of you may be questioning the efficacy of these results because they were compiled using back-tested data. To combat this, we've included a live example for good measure. This example is demonstrated using our Sterling Tactical Rotation Strategy, which launched on February 1, 2010, and has had its performance GIPS verified by Ashland Partners since its inception. From the launch date through December 31, 2015, the only asset class in our rotation that experienced a bear market was commodities. Through this period the PowerShares DB Commodity Tracking ETF (DBC) was down 41.11 percent. Through the same period, our strategy was allocated to commodities during eleven separate months, posting positive returns from our commodity exposure during a severe bear market.

CHAPTER 4

# Reinterpreting Asset Allocation

*If you have trouble imagining a 20 percent loss in the stock market, you shouldn't be in stocks.*

—John (Jack) Bogle

In chapter 3, we discussed the history of asset allocation and debunked the idea that no one has the ability to avoid some or most of bear markets by showing examples using US stocks and bonds and international equities. In this chapter we are going to tie everything up in a nice, tidy knot and show how combining these three asset classes into a pseudo asset-allocation portfolio could potentially outpace a more traditional, buy-and-hold asset-allocation model with significantly lower downside risk. Again, keep in mind that these returns do not include trading costs or taxes.

Let's make this as simple as possible. The majority of investors are either allocated to a 40/60 or a 60/40 asset-allocation model. This refers to the percentage of equities and bonds that make up an allocation. For instance, a 40/60 allocation invests 40 percent of assets in global equities and 60 percent in bonds. A 60/40 allocation consists of 60 percent equities and 40 percent bonds.

For the first simulation, let's use the Vanguard Conservative Growth mutual fund (VSCGX) as the 40/60 benchmark. This fund allocates 40 percent to equities and 60 percent to bonds and provides investors access to asset allocation with low costs. For the seven-MPC model we will allocate 28 percent to our US equity sleeve, 12 percent to our international equity sleeve, and 60 percent to our US bond sleeve. The performance for each was shown and discussed in chapter 3. This type of allocation is typical for a buy-and-hold asset-allocation model. Again, our rotations are either in the asset class or are sitting in a money-market account. The chart below shows the calendar-year performance of VSCGX and the seven-MPC model.

| Year | VSCGX | 7 MPC 40/60 |
|---|---|---|
| 2015 | -0.17% | -2.84% |
| 2014 | 6.95% | 5.51% |
| 2013 | 9.08% | 9.80% |
| 2012 | 9.19% | 12.01% |
| 2011 | 1.76% | 0.17% |
| 2010 | 11.14% | 5.07% |
| 2009 | 17.06% | 17.00% |
| 2008 | -19.52% | 2.66% |
| 2007 | 6.99% | 7.31% |
| 2006 | 10.62% | 9.62% |
| 2005 | 4.54% | 4.64% |
| 2004 | 8.02% | 7.43% |
| 2003 | 16.57% | 14.35% |
| 2002 | -4.10% | 1.76% |
| 2001 | -0.65% | 5.73% |
| 2000 | -2.65% | 3.29% |
| $100,000 | $195,790 | $268,819 |

## Create Wealth By Preserving Capital

During the 2000–2002 equity bear market, VSCGX (the buy-and-hold asset-allocation fund) dropped 6.24 percent, while the seven-MPC model was up 11.13 percent. During the 2008 equity bear market, VSCGX lost 19.52 percent, and the seven-MPC model posted a positive 2.66 percent return. Through the entire sixteen-year simulation, the seven-MPC model turned $100,000.00 into $268,000.00, while the asset-allocation mutual fund turned it into $195,000.00. As you can see from the chart above, most of the years outside the two bear markets were relatively similar between the two investing approaches. The outperformance came almost entirely from the seven-MPC model outperforming through the bear markets. This is a great example of how investors can create wealth by preserving capital through avoiding some or most bear markets.

It is interesting to note that, over the entire sixteen years, the seven-MPC model beat the buy-and-hold by $73,000.00. However, at the end of 2008, the seven-MPC model held a $56,000.00 lead: $172,000.00 versus $116,000.00 for the buy-and-hold allocation. The power of compounding from a much higher dollar amount did the rest of the work, as the seven-MPC model underperformed slightly between 2009 and 2015 but, in actual excess dollars, outperformed. We will be covering the power of compounding in a later chapter.

Also in a later chapter, we will be covering the fixed-income bear market that occurred from 1949 to 1981, which showed an example of a severe bond bear market. We mention this because the performance you see above took place during a bond bull market, and a 40/60 buy-and-hold asset-allocation model over the next decade will more than likely not perform anywhere near as well. The time has come to reevaluate your fixed-income investments and methodologies.

Using the same methodology that we used for the 40/60 portfolio above, let's take a look at how a 60/40 portfolio would do versus a buy-and-hold asset-allocation model. For the seven-MPC model, we will allocate 40 percent to the US-equity rotation sleeve, 20 percent to the international equity sleeve, and 40 percent to our bond rotation. For our benchmark we will use the Vanguard Balanced Index Fund (VBINX), which is a 60/40 allocation fund. Again, we are using the data from chapter 3 to determine the performance for each of the seven-MPC models, simply combining their returns into an asset-allocation model structure. These models are either 100 percent in the asset class or invested 100 percent to cash, based on the seven-month price change model. Below is a chart that details the performance data.

| Year | VBINX | 7 MPC 60/40 |
|---|---|---|
| 2015 | 0.37% | -3.57% |
| 2014 | 9.84% | 6.28% |
| 2013 | 17.91% | 16.01% |
| 2012 | 11.33% | 12.73% |
| 2011 | 4.14% | -1.04% |
| 2010 | 13.13% | 3.09% |
| 2009 | 20.05% | 18.53% |
| 2008 | -22.21% | 1.77% |
| 2007 | 6.16% | 7.16% |
| 2006 | 11.02% | 12.89% |
| 2005 | 4.65% | 5.72% |
| 2004 | 9.33% | 8.32% |
| 2003 | 19.87% | 19.08% |
| 2002 | -9.52% | -2.28% |
| 2001 | -3.02% | 3.82% |
| 2000 | -4.47% | -1.36% |
| $100,000 | $215,741 | $272,283 |

## Create Wealth By Preserving Capital

As you can see, the even MPC model did very well once again through both bear markets. It was up 0.73 percent during the 2000 through 2002 bear market versus a negative 16.1 percent for the VBINX benchmark. During the 2008 market collapse, the seven-MPC model posted a positive 1.77 percent return, while the benchmark was down 22.21 percent. During the entire sixteen-year simulation, $100,000.00 invested in the seven-MPC model would have grown to $272,283.00 and the benchmark to $215,741.00. Once again, the seven-MPC model performed better than a buy-and-hold asset-allocation model over the entire period and did so by producing positive returns during the two bear markets.

Both 60/40 allocations had four negative years; the difference was that the seven-MPC model's largest calendar-year loss was only 3.57 percent versus the 22.21 percent decline for the benchmark. The outperformance can be illustrated by taking the closing dollar valuations of each at the end of 2008. Beginning with $100,000.00, the seven-MPC model had grown to $168,000.00 at the end of 2008, while the benchmark buy-and-hold 60/40 asset-allocation model had only grown to $105,000.00. During the bull market that followed from 2009 to 2015, the benchmark made up some of the performance. During the first nine years of the simulation, the seven-MPC model had grown $63,000.00 more than the benchmark, and through the entire period it beat the benchmark by only $56,000.00. But that is the point at the end of the day. Performing well during bear markets is more important than outperforming during bull markets. Just ask the client we discussed in chapter 2. As you may recall, she turned $100,000.00 into $1,200,000.00 during the 1990s bull market, only to lose it all and then some during the bear market that followed. When the account was shut down, it had been decimated to $50,000.00.

At this point one might come to the conclusion that we are not fans of asset allocation. Well, that's not entirely true. After bad-mouthing asset allocation over the past couple of chapters, let's switch gears for a moment. There are many benefits to including buy-and-hold asset allocations in an overall portfolio. Doing so significantly lowers tax exposure, especially when tax-free municipal bonds are included in the allocation. Also, when setting up an asset-allocation model using low-cost ETFs, investors can put together portfolios that keep costs down. While both the 60/40 and 40/60 asset-allocation models lost money during the two bear markets, they still significantly outperformed the S&P 500 during those periods.

Our contention is that asset-allocation models serve a purpose in an overall portfolio but should not be the only investment methodology that is put to use. Instead, we view them as a base in an overall financial plan. The percentage of a portfolio that is allocated to asset allocation should be well thought out and designed around the risk tolerance and unique circumstances of each individual client and should take seriously the idea of *mean reversion*.

We believe asset-allocation models that remain static through full economic and market cycles are not the best solution for most investors. There is a theory called mean reversion that states that all asset classes will eventually revert back to their long-term mean or average. Employing this deep into a bull or bear market can substantially increase returns over full cycles and has the potential to limit downside exposure. Let's take a look at how this might be employed today.

The S&P 500 has been enjoying a historically long and fruitful bull market over the past eighty-nine months and, as of August 23, 2016, was at 2,192. It fell as low as 667 during the depths of the Great Recession in March 2009. A simple way to calculate the mean or average of the S&P 500 during this bull market would be to add the monthly adjusted closing prices for the S&P 500 and then divide by the number of months. Using this formula, the mean for the S&P 500 on August 23, 2016, was 1,552, or 29.19 percent above the average price of the past eighty-nine monthly closes. We are well aware that at this time equity markets were significantly above their mean and that at some point in the future, they will revert back to their mean.

We also realize that equity markets often move higher and lower and last longer in both directions than anyone expects. How could a prudent investor use the current market environment to help protect his or her portfolio? In this scenario the best outcome would be to remain fully invested with equity exposure within one's asset-allocation model while applying an exit strategy. This would give an investor the opportunity to profit if the markets continued higher and a succinct sell price to protect his or her gains.

We are going to apply a simple technical strategy to remain fully invested until a reversal in price becomes a statistically higher probability. To do this we are going to look at the last two breakouts of the S&P 500 that took the index in new all-time highs. The first occurred in May 2015 when the S&P 500 hit an all-time high of 2,134. It took until July of 2016 for the S&P 500 to break through that price, again reconfirming the bull market. We would be looking at 2,120 as the exit price for some or all of an investor's equity exposure, which is 3.28 percent below where the market is trading at the time of this writing.

The reason these two breakouts are so important is mostly due to human emotions. Behavioral science in investing shows that many investors who buy near the top and then witness their investments falling in value will often wait for them to come back to breakeven and then sell them. This is the primary reason that it often takes multiple days for an equity market to break through crucial resistance levels, as more selling among spooked investors take place during these periods. Once the market breaks through resistance, the additional selling abates, and equities often move higher. Conversely, sellers usually multiply once key support is broken. In this case support has been built up in the 2,130 range.

When selling directly below support, there is a keen possibility that this could lead to what is called being whipsawed. Being whipsawed is selling once an asset class or stock breaks through support and having to buy it back at a slightly higher price should it move back through resistance. At this point in the extended bull market, if applied effectively, this exit strategy could have a profound impact on the

## Create Wealth By Preserving Capital

portfolio through a full market cycle. However, it should be combined with other strategies in a full asset allocation. The idea is to limit downside exposure. This reminds me of when Warren Buffet was asked what his best advice regarding investing was and said, "Rule number one is to never lose money, and rule number two, never forget rule number one." Sage advice from a wise and outrageously successful investing legend.

Mean reversion is a technique that can be applied when asset classes become overly extended during long bull markets but will also help decide which asset classes have become undervalued according to their mean or average prices during severe bear markets.

In the fall of 2011, all anyone could talk about was the price of gold. Financial magazines, newspapers, CNBC, and their ilk devoted much of their time to the skyrocketing price of gold and rightfully so. The SPDR Gold Shares ETF (GLD) closed out 2004 at $43.00. By September 2011 it had hit an all-time high of $185.00 and then began to reverse and spiral all the way back down to a low of $100.00 in December 2015. This represented a steep discount to the mean reversion metrics we utilize at Sterling Global Strategies, and we began to watch for a breakout through resistance. This breakout occurred on February 19th, 2016, a day that GLD traded as high as $117.97. We bought ETFS Swiss Gold ETF (SGOL) that day, as there were no trading costs associated with it. We used GLD as our example above because it had an additional five years of live trading. Both ETFs track the price of gold.

## Mark W. Eicker

In summary, we believe that reimagining asset allocation by utilizing multiple strategies within a portfolio helps mitigate downside risk in an allocation. Traditional buy-and-hold asset allocating works just fine, but there are tools available that can make the concept even more effective and powerful.

CHAPTER 5

# Disco, Oil Embargo, and Gold: The Wild 1970s

> It was the biggest inflation and the most sustained inflation that the United States has ever had.
>
> —Paul A. Volcker

As I was born in 1970, the decade encompassed my formidable years, and most of what I've learned about the time period, I learned through reading. One of my first memories in life, however, took place in the back of one of our two Ford LTDs (not that kind of memory), with my sister sitting next to me and my mom and dad in the front. Twice a week, we would load into one of the cars and head to the nearest gas station. One of our license plates ended in an even number, which allowed us to fill up the gas tank on Monday, Wednesday, Friday, or Sunday. The other car's license plate ended in an odd number, which meant we could fill that car up on Tuesday,

Thursday, or Saturday. This was during the oil embargo, and the government had decided on this system of even and odd license plates in an attempt to ration gasoline. I also remember the occasional gas station sign that read, "Temporarily Closed, We're Out of Gas."

Sometimes we would get lucky and only have a few cars in front of us at the gas station when we arrived. Other times, the line would curl around the block, and cars would be lined up on the boulevard, causing ongoing traffic to snarl to a halt as two lanes turned into one. I remember horns honking angrily, shouting matches among irritated customers in line, and the unrelenting heat of a California desert sun pounding down on a car with no air conditioning. I also remember hearing conversations that bordered on despair coming from the front seat.

I come from a humble upbringing. My dad was a bartender, and my mom was a homemaker. Money was tight and becoming tighter, as inflation was rising rapidly. My parents often discussed money in the front seat and how they could cut costs. Gasoline, food, clothing, and medical costs were moving higher, and my parents' income was basically fixed.

My dad drove fifty miles round trip to work, and his car was a gas guzzler. He refused to buy the Toyotas and Hondas that were rapidly becoming popular because of their fuel efficiency. My dad was going to buy American no matter what, but the high gasoline prices were becoming ever more burdensome. Spending cuts had to be made over and over again to keep up with the rising prices.

## Create Wealth By Preserving Capital

The government, on the other hand, was spending like drunken sailors during the latter half of the 1960s. The Vietnam War was sucking the coffers dry, and Lyndon Baines Johnson was spending generously on the Great Society. The Great Society was implemented by LBJ as a war on poverty, and many of its social programs remain today, such as Medicare and Medicaid, the Older Americans Act, and federal education funding, Pell grants, and loans. These programs would expand during the early 1970s under the leadership of Richard Nixon. While admirable programs, they would contribute, along with many central bank and government missteps, to the rising interest rates and inflationary decade that followed their introduction.

Unemployment in the United States hit an all-time low of 1.2 percent during World War II in 1944. The recession of 1960 lasted for ten months, and unemployment had spiked to 7.1 percent in May of 1961. This spurred President John F. Kennedy to increase Social Security and implement stimulus spending. Sound familiar? Governments, based on Keynesian economics, like to spend their way out of recessions, and 1960 was no different.

Richard Nixon would later say that the recession had cost him the election. He had been running against JFK as the sitting vice president, and JFK effectively used the recession as ammunition during the debates. The fact that these debates were the first to be televised and Nixon sweated profusely during them could also have caused him to lose to the more affable and charismatic JFK.

## Mark W. Eicker

In 1964 LBJ, having been sworn in as president after the assassination of JFK, cut taxes across the board for individuals and corporations, which would lead to substantial economic growth during the next few years. Gross national product grew by 7 percent in 1964, 8 percent in 1965, and 9 percent in 1966, which was incredibly robust growth. One economist commented that this period represented the best economic prosperity during the postwar recovery.

LBJ decided not to run for a second full term, and Richard Nixon was sworn in as president in January 1969. As mentioned earlier, LBJ was funding the war and widespread social programs through budget deficits. Nixon would ramp up the spending following the 1970 recession, which he inherited from LBJ. Nixon was considered a fiscal conservative; however, in practice he was not. Like LBJ before him, Nixon ran budget deficits that would eventually spook dollar investors overseas.

The Federal Reserve chairman during this period was Arthur Burns. While many economists of the day believed that inflation could be controlled through monetary policy (tightening money supply), Arthur Burns did not. He believed that inflation was caused by wage-cost pressures, and if this were the case, tightening money supply would be a useless tool to implement. It was his belief that the economy and inflation were driven by unions and that higher pay rippled through the economy and caused inflation. For instance, an auto union wins a big increase in pay for its members, and this triggers the other unions to demand higher pay. Automakers would then lay off workers and raise prices for the cars they sold to make up for additional employment costs. With this happening across the country in innumerable industries, inflation would be constant, and monetary policy would have no impact on controlling it.

At the same time, the Nixon administration was running an expansionary economic policy and advocated dealing with inflation through wage and price controls. Nixon was running for reelection, and believing he had lost his presidential bid in 1960 because the election fell during a recession, he was more concerned with keeping unemployment low than with controlling inflation. Even with inflation rising, his administration continued to run significant budget deficits, which fueled money supply. The money supply grew from $710 billion in 1971 to $802 billion in 1972, setting the scene for the inflation fire to come.

Obviously, the easy money policies of the central bank, which were designed to generate full employment, were partly to blame for the inflation that resulted. However, there were other villains that played vital roles in an inflation rate that more than doubled to 8.8 percent in 1973 and eventually topped out above 14 percent during 1980.

Representatives from forty-four nations met in Bretton Woods, New Hampshire, to develop a new international monetary system that came to be known as the Bretton Woods system. Countries under the system settled their international accounts using dollars that could be converted to gold at a fixed rate of $35.00, which was guaranteed by the US government.

It worked well for a while, until 1965, when France broke away from the system because it felt America was the only beneficiary. By 1971 the money supply had grown to the point at which the United States did not have enough gold to back the system. West Germany left next, then Switzerland, and the United States made the ill-fated decision to end Bretton Woods. In an attempt to prevent a run on the dollar, Nixon imposed an import surcharge of 10 percent. He then froze wages and prices for ninety days. Finally, he suspended the convertibility of the dollar into gold.

The dollar had become a fiat currency, and the old Bretton Woods gold-backed system turned into the floating of currencies that remains today. The dollar plunged more than 35 percent during the 1970s, causing dollar-denominated commodities such as oil to skyrocket. Immediately following the announcement, the dollar began to plunge, and Japan, Germany, and many other central banks began to buy the dollar to prevent a free fall.

The wage-price controls forced companies to keep wages high, which meant businesses laid off workers to reduce costs. To make matters worse, they couldn't lower prices to stimulate demand, which also fell. The Federal Reserve raised and lowered interest rates so many times that businesses were unable to plan for the future. As a result, they kept prices high, worsening inflation.

## Create Wealth By Preserving Capital

Many folks blame the OPEC oil embargo on the Israel-Egypt war, often referred to as the Yom Kippur War. The United States supported Israel in the war, and OPEC decided it had had enough and stopped shipping oil to the United States. In all truth that was probably the last straw after the United States came off the gold standard. Ending Bretton Woods caused the dollar to plummet, which really hurt OPEC countries whose oil contracts were priced in US dollars. In either case the result was having the price of oil rise from an inflation-adjusted price of $19.49 in March 1973 to $51.44 in January 1974 and ultimately to top out in April of 1980 at an unfathomable price of $115.62 per barrel. That's nearly a 600 percent move higher for oil over a seven-year period.

As one can see, many factors played a role in the inflationary 1970s saga: ongoing budget deficits, a departure from the gold standard, price and wage controls, and finally oil. The price of oil affects nearly all products produced and shipped. Whether by rail, truck, plane, or ship, it costs more to move everything when oil prices are high. To recoup costs, manufacturers raised prices on nearly everything, from milk and butter to automobiles.

The graph below shows the history of interest rates in the United States from 1790 through 2012, using the ten-year Treasury bond yield. The graph shows that interest rates for the ten-year bonds hit an all-time low in 1945 during World War II. Sixty-seven years later they made a new historical low in 2012. As of this writing, they remain near their historical lows.

## Mark W. Eicker

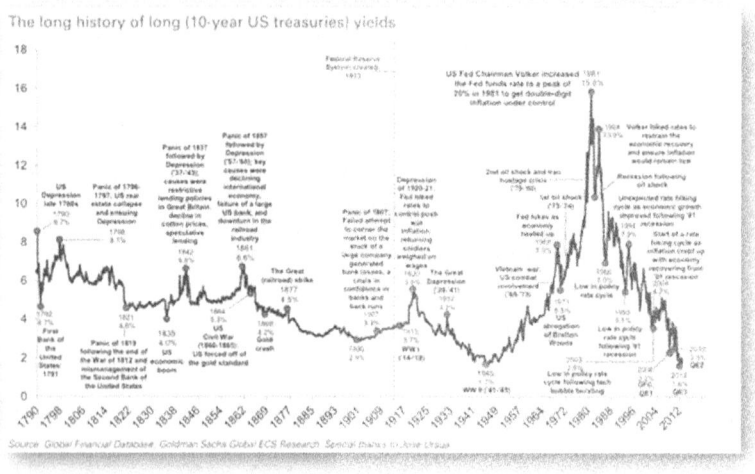

The bear market for bonds began in 1946 but accelerated during the 1970s and did not officially end until 1981, when Federal Chairman Paul Volker raised the federal fund rate to 20 percent, which choked off inflation. This represents a thirty-five-year bond bear market, followed by a bond bull market that has lasted thirty-five years through 2016. The graph from 1945 to 2012 has great symmetry, almost like looking in the mirror. Straight up and then straight back down.

What is the downside risk for a fixed-income investor during a severe bond bear market? One of the few fixed-income mutual funds that was around back in the 1970s and is still being managed as of this writing is the Vanguard Wellesley Income mutual fund (VWINX). It was launched on July 1, 1970, and while it owns mostly fixed-income instruments, such as Treasury and corporate bonds, it also invests in high-quality, dividend-producing equities to a lesser extent. VWINX was trading at $13.15 on November 30, 1972, and had dropped to $9.32 by the end of September 1974. During this twenty-two-month period, the fixed-income mutual fund lost 29.12 percent of its value.

While severe losses in bonds are rare, during a period of rising interest rates, bonds will not provide the same type of counterbalance to a portfolio that they do when interest rates are falling. For example, from July 31, 1970, through March 31, 1980, VWINX fell more than 15 percent. Compare those losses to the bond market from February 28, 2009, through February 28, 2015, and you will quickly understand the difficulty of asset allocating when interest rates are rising. VWINX was up 55.48 percent during this six-year time period.

We know what you are thinking. The 1970s were a different period, and this will never happen again, right? Well, the 1970s were definitely nothing like today, but that doesn't mean that the grand experiment that the Federal Reserve is conducting (quantitative easing / dovish monetary policies) won't eventually lead to rising interest rates and inflation. The world is awash in money like never before. The entire world is attempting to avoid a global recession/depression by printing money and keeping interest rates low. Some central banks have taken their key interest rates negative in an attempt to force banks to lend and create an environment that promotes inflation. The question remains: Can we trust the Federal Reserve and central banks around the world not to make any mistakes while operating in uncharted territory? If there are missteps, will they look different from what happened during the 1970s?

There is a growing body of academic research that suggests keeping interest rates low will not create growth because companies realize they will be able to borrow at low interest rates in the future, so there is no reason to speed up capital expenditures. This theory flies in the face of conventional economic thought and suggests that growth and inflation will only pick up once central banks telegraph that they will be raising their key interest rates at a methodical and consistent pace. By doing so, corporations will be forced to spend money today at lower interest rates. If central banks were to adopt this theory as policy, no one could possibly predict with any statistical probability what would happen because it has never been done before.

Let's end this chapter by looking at how the seven-MPC model would have held up during the bond bear market of the 1970s. We will use the Vanguard Wellesley Income fund (VWINX) as the benchmark and also the fund we will rotate between for the seven-MPC model. Since VWINX launched in July 1970, we will start with the first date we can use for data, which is February 28, 1971, and take the simulation through March 31, 1980. Through this period VWINX was down 20.22 percent, and although the seven-MPC model also lost money, it held up much better, only losing 6.29 percent.

CHAPTER 6

# Behavioral Economics Theory

> The four most dangerous words in investing
> are: "this time it's different."
>
> —Sir John Templeton

It has been more than seven years since the devastating bear market of 2008 came to an end during March 2009. From top to bottom, US equities fell more than 50 percent and took a toll on the nation's psyche. News headlines of the day began referring to 401(k)s as 201(k)s, as many accounts had their value cut in half. There were bank failures and news reports of folks lining up early in front of their banks to withdraw their hard-earned cash. For a while it appeared that the entire system was going to break down. The Federal Reserve stepped in and turned chaos into calm, and investors came back to the markets.

Unfortunately, many people did not come out of the recession unscathed. Many people were left without jobs, and some of them remain out of work or are underemployed to this day. The economy barely escaped another Great Depression; the last one was a dark period for Americans, as many were left without food, hope, or employment. The images of people queued up in soup lines and milling around cities during the 1930s are freeze-framed in our public consciousness.

While we are only seven years removed from the devastation caused by the 2008–2009 equity bear market, many investors have become complacent. That happens during long bull markets and can be explained by behavioral economics. *Recency bias* and *herd mentality* are the terms used to explain this phenomenon. The more time that goes by, the less investors are fearful of the event reoccurring.

Back in the 1950s, prior to the study of behavioral economics, traditional economics conceptualized a world populated by calculating, unemotional investors. The standard economic model was based on investors being rational, instituting willpower, and inherently acting in a self-serving manner.

In contrast to the standard economic model, investors are often irrational in their decision-making. Humans have only so much time and brainpower, and therefore people often adopt rules of thumb when making decisions. During the late 1990s, investors who had made money on one technology stock would often buy another one, not taking the time to learn anything about the company but expecting it to go up because the last technology stock they owned did. Departures from rationality emerge both in judgments and in choices; some examples include overconfidence, optimism, and fear.

## Create Wealth By Preserving Capital

To highlight irrational behavior, I point to a 1990s study of New York City taxi drivers. The taxi company that employed these drivers charged them a fixed price to drive the cabs for each shift, typically twelve hours, and the driver kept whatever was left over at the end of the day. The driver decided how long he would work each day. If the driver wanted to maximize profits, the best strategy would be to work longer on the good days (when conventions were in town, rainy days, etc.) and to work less on the bad days. However, the irrational mind made most of the taxi drivers do the exact opposite. They looked at each day as profitable or nonprofitable and typically worked longer hours on the bad days and fewer hours on the good days. This same irrationality can make investors sell their winners too soon and hold on to their losers.

The second tenet of traditional economics is that investors in the equity markets display complete self-control. Behavioral science tells us this is not the case. If the human race exhibited complete self-control, we would all avoid the things that are bad for us. We should all recognize that eating too much, drinking too much, smoking cigarettes, saving, and exercising too little (and the list could go on) are bad for us. However, there are billions of people around the world practicing habits that they know are bad because humans as a whole lack self-control, just as investors do.

The third tenet of traditional economics is that investors are self-serving. Behavioral finance would point out that, from 2004 to 2014, at least 50 percent of all households in the United States contributed some money to charity each year, with the average dollar amount approaching 2 percent of household income. This flies in the face of traditional economics, which thrives on the belief that humans' primary motive is self-interest and that individuals cannot be expected to contribute to the public good unless their private welfare is improved by their actions.

A friend of mine who works in the medical field invests only in socially responsible mutual funds. When she told her adviser that she did not want to own any companies that were tied to oil, weapons, tobacco, alcohol, and such, her adviser asked her if she wanted to make money. Her response was that she wanted to make money if the socially responsible companies she invested in made her money; otherwise the answer was no. This runs counter to the traditional economic model that assumes every investor is completely self-serving and only makes investment decisions based on how they affect his or her life.

Albert Einstein once said that the definition of insanity is doing the same thing over and over again and expecting a different outcome. However, behavioral finance shows that investors tend to fall into patterns of destructive behavior. They continue to do the same things over and over again, expecting different outcomes. In the rest of the chapter, we will outline the mistakes that many investors continue to make time and again.

Many investors damage their portfolios by underdiversifying. As I'm writing this, the FAANG stocks are still very popular with retail investors. These companies are Facebook, Apple, Amazon, Netflix, and Google. All are very well-run companies

## Create Wealth By Preserving Capital

with enviable business models. However, valuations appear to be a concern with a number of these equity darlings.

Facebook (FB) went public at $38.00 per share on May 18, 2012, and fell to $18.00 per share in September 2012. Since then, it has soared more than 700 percent to $126.12 on August 31, 2016. As of this writing, the price-to-earnings ratio (PE) is 62.41. This means the company earns $1,600.00 for every $100,000.00 invested in its stock. Should growth begin to slow, the stock could suffer.

Apple (AAPL) traded at $17.98 per share at the beginning of this bull market on April 30, 2009. The stock had risen 580 percent to $106.10 by August 31, 2016. While the appreciation has been remarkable, the stock trades at a below-market valuation of 12.45 times earnings.

Amazon (AMZN), on the other hand, trades at an astronomical valuation of 195 times earnings. The stock skyrocketed 850 percent from $80.52 in April 2009 to $769.16 in August 2016. Investors in this stock had better hope that Amazon executes its business plan flawlessly and that there remains an appetite for risk.

Netflix (NFLX) has catapulted more than 1,500 percent during this bull market, and as of this writing, its PE ratio sits at more than 300 times earnings. How many of you would pay $100,000.00 for only $333.00 worth of earnings? Earnings would have to double, then double again, and then nearly double once more for NFLX to trade at 10 times earnings. Could it happen? Of course, but this is an extremely rich valuation by any metric.

## Mark W. Eicker

Google's (GOOG) share price has increased by 388 percent during this bull market, and the valuation at the time of this writing is at 30 times earnings. While the valuation for Google is richer than the overall equity market, it might be justified.

Benjamin Graham and many others after him have said that as soon as there is an acronym for stocks, it is time to sell. This line of thinking takes into account the herd mentality and the fact that once an acronym is used to describe a set of stocks, the trade has become crowded. Too often, retail investors fall in love with the glamour stocks, stop looking at valuations, and revert to only looking at the names.

The main problem with the FAANG stocks is not that they are overvalued but that there are many investors who own a high percentage of these names and are not properly diversifying. These equities are highly correlated and will likely rise and fall in unison.

Other common mistakes that investors make include loss aversion, in which the fear of losing money leads to a withdrawal of capital at the worst possible time. This is also known as panic selling. Anchoring is remaining focused on what happened previously and not adapting to a changing market. Mental accounting is separating performance of investments mentally to justify successes and failures. Herding is following what everyone else is doing, which leads to crowded trades and buying high / selling low. The FAANG trade is an example of herding. Making overly optimistic assumptions tends to lead to dramatic reversions when the assumptions are met with reality. And finally, media response ties in with optimism as a mistake investors make. The media has a bias toward optimism to sell products for sponsors and advertisers and also attract viewership.

The research firm Dalbar & Associates conducts an annual Quantitative Analysis of Investor Behavior study that looks at how an average investor performs versus the S&P 500. The study found that equity investor returns over the three-year period ending December 31, 2015, trailed the S&P 500 by more than 6 percent annually. The five-year period was not much better, as they annualized 5.5 percent less than the S&P 500 and 3.5 percent less annually during the twenty-year period. The average investor trailed by nearly 7 percent during the thirty-year period.

These are all time periods during which bonds were experiencing a historic bull market. As of this writing, we stand at the precipice of a record high bond and equity market. The 60/40 asset-allocation models have performed much better than they will during a bond bear market. There is the likelihood that, in the coming months or years, a bond bear market will coincide with an equity bear market and force many risk-averse investors to sell at precisely the wrong juncture. History has shown us that when investors sell low, it often takes years for them to trust the markets and get back in.

Institutional investors avoid the mistakes that retail investors make by following strict investment methodologies that force them to follow processes. This takes the emotional aspects of investing out of the picture and in turn generally improves performance over full market cycles. It can be extremely difficult to follow processes long term because there will invariably be periods of underperformance. Sticking with the firm's investment methodology isn't always easy, but it remains the best solution.

We believe there is a better way to preserve wealth than simply buying and holding a traditional asset-allocation model. In the upcoming chapters, we will look at different models that we believe can be utilized within an asset-allocation model to help mitigate downside exposure during both equity and bond bear markets.

CHAPTER 7

# The Evolution of Rotation Theory

> You get recessions, you have stock market declines. If you don't understand that's going to happen, then you're not ready, you won't do well in the markets.
>
> —PETER LYNCH

ACADEMICS AND PORTFOLIO managers are continually testing new and evolving methodologies to produce investment strategies that improve existing risk/reward parameters for investment portfolios. They understand there are many paths to achieving positive long-term performance. They are also aware that many investors underestimate their tolerance for volatility, which is a major contributor to overall investor underperformance.

As mentioned earlier, Dalbar Inc., an independent 401(k) research firm, has produced numerous studies showing that the average 401(k) participant not only underperforms the markets but does so by a significant margin. The company's research found that the major contributor to participant underperformance was selling at or near market bottoms and failing to reenter the equity markets until they had fully recovered. This is the classic "chase the hot dot" mentality that we discussed in chapter 1.

Even the most seasoned investor is more comfortable during bull markets. We all love to see our portfolios rising in value, but we often forget that outperformance and true wealth creation can also be attained during bear markets. Avoiding bear markets was the driver of outperformance for the seven-MPC portfolios that we tested in chapters 3 and 4.

Rotation theory was developed to significantly limit downside losses during bear markets and to provide in-line returns during bull markets, the exact opposite of traditional money management. The vast majority of mutual fund and portfolio managers strive to outperform during bull markets, while slightly outperforming during bear markets. Their approach is to slightly tweak their allocations to the benchmark they are attempting to beat with fairly high correlations to that benchmark.

The goal of this chapter is to articulate the history and evolution of rotation theory and how it can be a driving force in the pursuit of long-term outperformance. The most important contributors to rotation theory are modern portfolio theory (MPT) and momentum investing. Rotation theory essentially merges the best attribute of both theories and attempts to minimize their shortcomings. Some firms, including Sterling Global Strategies, have taken rotation theory to a new level by combining it with a go-to-cash option. We believe that having the ability to go to cash when most asset classes are falling in unison is a vital option for managing risk. The growth of the global economy has increased the chances of all asset classes dropping at the same time, essentially eliminating the benefit of both MPT and momentum investing. The idea behind including a go-to-cash option is best summed up by the popular Wall Street saying "The best time to invest is when there is blood in the streets." Knowing when to go to cash and, more importantly, when to reinvest becomes the question.

Modern portfolio theory has its benefits as well as its shortcomings. We've discussed in previous chapters that Dr. Harry Markowitz first introduced this theory in 1952. He postulated in his paper that combing three asset classes—bonds, international equities, and domestic equities—would reduce volatility while generating the greatest possible return for each unit of risk.

The concept behind MPT is that low-correlated asset classes often move in different directions. By combining bonds, international equities, and domestic equities (which exhibited low correlations to one another back in 1952), investors would experience fewer extremes. For instance, in any given year, if bonds were up 5 percent, international equities were up 15 percent, domestic equities fell 10 percent, and a portfolio was constructed 40/20/40, respectively. Then that investment portfolio would return a positive 1 percent for the year, avoiding the 10 percent loss that investors singularly investing in domestic equities would have taken. Taking MPT in its simplest form, its investors will never perform as well as the top-performing asset class, nor will they ever perform as poorly as the worst-performing asset class. They will always perform somewhere in the middle.

Through the years, the three asset classes initially proposed by Dr. Harry Markowitz became increasingly correlated, reducing the effectiveness of MPT. Since the 1980s, additional low or even negatively correlated asset classes have been brought to market to mimic the investment profile that MPT enjoyed during those early years. But even some of these specialized asset classes have become more correlated to one another and to the broad markets over time. Today, most academics and portfolio constructors utilize obscure asset classes such as currencies, equity futures, timbre, precious metals, inverse or shorting mechanisms, and real estate in their search to recreate the correlations and portfolio protection that MPT exhibited early on.

MPT has one minor flaw that we believe can be manipulated. MPT requires that multiple asset classes be combined no matter which direction the asset class is going. The very essence of the theory is that no one can predict when an asset class is in a bear market or when it is in a bull market. Therefore, one needs to own every asset class in various percentages all the time. We simply do not agree with this contention.

Asset classes go through very consistent bull markets, which are then followed by bear markets. Each asset class experiences this phenomenon, but some asset classes have historically stayed in bear markets for longer periods than others. US equities, for instance, have averaged somewhere around a twelve-month bear market since 1950. International equities

## Create Wealth By Preserving Capital

have averaged around fourteen months, commodities have averaged about seven years, and US bonds have lasted on average nearly eighteen years.

While we know of no process that can avoid a bear market in its entirety, we do believe we have created an algorithm that can avoid most of a bear market. In our Sterling tactical rotation strategy, which we launched on February 1, 2010, the only asset class that we rotate between that has experienced a bear market is commodities. We not only avoided most of the commodity bear market, but our exposure to the asset class produced positive returns. Up to this point, that is the only example we can give using live performance, but we believe we will be able to avoid the majority of the next equity bear market as well. Only time will tell. Our investment methodology uses momentum as a means to avoid weak-performing asset classes.

George Chestnutt is considered by many to be the godfather of momentum investing. He began publishing market letters in the 1950s that ranked both stocks and industries based on their relative strengths. Sound familiar? Chestnutt used his relative-strength models to manage the highly successful no-load mutual fund American Investors Trust, which experienced the best mutual-fund track record of the 1960s before fizzling out in the 1970s.

Since then, numerous studies have been conducted on momentum investing. There is conclusive evidence that momentum investing leads to outperformance over full market cycles, leading most academics to convert to believers over the past five decades. The research published in a 1993 paper by

## Mark W. Eicker

Narasimhan Jegadesh and Sheridan Titmann titled "Returns to Buying Winners and Selling Losers: Implications for Stock Market Efficiency" proved that momentum strategies based solely on historical pricing data outperformed over time.

During the mid-2000s, two finance professors set out to try to determine why momentum investing worked so well. Jacob Sagi, with the help of Mark Seasholes, professors at the Haas School of Business at the University of California, Berkeley, set out to determine if the momentum outperformance phenomenon was the result of market inefficiencies and irrational investor behavior, as many practitioners at the time believed. Their groundbreaking study was published in *The Journal of Financial Economics*. Jacob Sagi said, "Our results indicate that the success of momentum strategies is not about market inefficiency and low risk but appears to be tied directly to specific attributes of a company that affect the way its risk varies over time." 1

Sagi believes that his research shows that the outperformance of momentum investing may be associated with higher risk attributes. "Our model economy was made up of firms doing economically rational things in a rational market, and the study's results point toward the possibility that momentum may not be giving investors high return with low risk after all."

In theory, momentum investing is designed to buy the stocks or asset classes that are appreciating the fastest during bull markets and then to begin buying the stocks or asset classes that are falling the most slowly during bear markets. Typically, a relative strength calculation of between three and twelve months is applied to a broad range of equities or asset classes, and those with the highest relative-strength scores are bought and held for a predetermined period of time. The biggest drawback to momentum investing is that the methodology can significantly underperform during bear markets as volatility picks up. Merging MPT with momentum investing and adding a go-to-cash element can help solve this problem.

Rotation theory (RT) essentially combines the best qualities of both MPT and momentum investing while actively attempting to avoid the worst-performing asset classes. It relies on low-correlated asset classes, just like MPT, and it utilizes relative strength in a similar manner to momentum investing.

The main difference between MPT and rotation theory is RT's ability to avoid the worst-performing asset classes, statistically speaking. Modern portfolio theory is based on the belief that no one can predict which asset classes are going to rise or fall, and therefore, it is imperative to own a piece of many asset classes. Rotation theory not only suggests that it is possible to predict which asset classes are in bear markets, but also indicates that it is critical to identify those lagging asset classes in order to experience outperformance over full market cycles while significantly lowering portfolio volatility.

CHAPTER 8

# Preserving Wealth

> Investing is for wealth preservation, not wealth creation, so first you have to make wealth.
>
> —James Altucher

Although there are numerous investment possibilities pertaining to wealth preservation, each strategy has its own set of shortcomings. Many conservative investors turn to CDs, US Treasury bonds, or AAA-insured municipal bonds to preserve wealth. Each of these options is a prudent investment choice; however, after adjusting for inflation and taxes, these investments provide little or even negative absolute returns. For the ultrarich this may not be problematic, as they have accumulated far more assets than they will ever spend. Most high-net-worth investors, unfortunately, can't be as laissez-faire about their investment portfolios as the ultrarich. Living off a retirement portfolio that is not keeping up with inflation and taxes can have dire consequences over a twenty- to thirty-year retirement. A $1,500,000.00 portfolio invested at 3 percent, with

## Create Wealth By Preserving Capital

a $75,000.00 per year spend rate adjusted for 3 percent inflation will deplete in less than twenty years. There are only three cures for this ailment: spend significantly less, seek higher investment returns, or die before the money runs out.

Monte Carlo is a retirement-simulation software program that can be utilized to determine the probability of retirement assets lasting a certain number of years, taking into account investment returns, inflation, taxes, and probable spending rates. Monte Carlo runs hundreds of thousands of simulations to determine its probabilities. For those of you nearing or in retirement who haven't had a Monte Carlo simulation run for you, it would be wise. It is much easier to adjust spending rates and investment options early on than after an investment portfolio begins to fail, at which time spending cuts are generally lifestyle changing.

Asset allocation is often the preferred wealth preservation strategy utilized by investment professionals. Asset allocation is based on the modern portfolio theories developed by Dr. Harry Markowitz in the 1950s. The strategy relies on asset classes exhibiting low correlations to one another, allowing them to move in opposite directions. It is usually explained by saying that some asset classes are going up and some are going down; if you own a piece of all of them, your performance will be somewhere in the middle, limiting the volatility of your investments. Recently, asset classes have become more correlated, limiting the positive impact asset allocation has previously displayed. As our world turns more toward a global economy, we should expect typical asset classes preferred for asset-allocation models to become increasingly more correlated and, therefore, less useful in reducing risk. The year 2008 was a great example of how a global economy can have negative effects on all asset classes, causing the vast majority of them to fall in unison. The past ten years have not been kind to asset-allocation models, and we believe that is going to continue to be the case as our world continues to become more connected. As Bob Dylan once sang, "The times, they are a-changing."

Annuities are also commonly used to preserve wealth. There are obvious shortcomings associated with annuities. High fees eat away at performance gains, limiting their upside potential. They tend to be illiquid investments, resulting in the need to have other investments as emergency funds. Annuities are also taxed as income, which can result in higher taxes than other investment choices.

We at Sterling Global Strategies believe using a combination of investment methodologies produces a more robust and less volatile portfolio. We strongly believe that including a tactical allocation to an investment portfolio over full market cycles will provide better returns and dampen volatility. We also contend that utilizing cash as an asset class at the correct times can help create wealth by preserving capital.

Morningstar has created its own database for tactical managers, which they call Managed ETF Strategists and which has been the fastest-growing segment it covers for a number of years. The ETF strategists vary widely in terms of their investment methodologies, but most are focused on reducing downside exposure during bear markets while attempting to capture upside as the equity markets rise. Some, like the Sterling tactical rotation strategy, attempt to rotate away from asset classes that are experiencing prolonged bear markets and can allocate 100 percent of assets to cash during markets when all asset classes are falling in unison.

Broad asset classes experience varying lengths of time in both bull and bear market cycles. US interest-rate cycles, which determine US Treasury bond cycles, last the longest of any asset class. For instance, over the past 218 years there have been four secular bull markets and three bear markets. The shortest interest-rate cycle was the twenty-two-year bear market between 1898 and 1920, and the longest bear market lasted thirty-five years between 1946 and 1981, which then began the second-longest interest rate bull market, which has lasted an additional thirty-five years through 2016. The point is that avoiding asset classes during bear markets can significantly improve risk-adjusted returns. The longer the cycle lasts, the easier it is to avoid.

US equity bull and bear market cycles are shorter than fixed-income cycles but can also be potentially avoided by rotating away from weakness and into strength. The average bull market for US equities lasts forty-seven months, while the average bear market swallows up thirteen months of performance. Avoiding the majority of an equity bear market can be crucial. If a portfolio falls 40 percent during a bear market, it takes a positive return of 66 percent just to get back to breakeven.

There are fits and starts to all asset classes during both bull and bear markets. They are never a straight line, and volatility is generally accentuated during bear markets. Utilizing tactical managers within an asset-allocation model can provide a buffer for the overall portfolio.

The Sterling tactical rotation strategy looks at six separate asset classes and equally weights the top two using a proprietary algorithm. The six asset classes are US and international equities, US bonds, REITs, commodities, and cash. The strategy is designed to perform well during both bull and bear markets.

Another strategy that can be implemented to potentially limit losses for an overall asset-allocation model is equity-linked notes, which can be customized to meet an investor's overall risk/return objective. These notes are constructed using options contracts and are typically tied to two separate indexes. The worst-performing of the two indexes is the return that the investor will receive. For instance, a note could be tied to both the Russell 2000 and the S&P 500. These notes have a maturity date associated with them. In this example, let's say it is three years. The example note will capture 102 percent of the upside. Therefore, if the Russell 2000 is up 60 percent on the maturity date, and the S&P 500 is up 40 percent, then the note would pay 40.8 percent above the purchase price or 102 percent of the increase.

Let's take a look at what happens to this example equity-linked note if the worst-performing of the two indexes is negative. This note has an absolute return barrier of 30 percent. What does that mean exactly? It is both protection and potential positive performance during a negative equity market, up to a buffer of a 30 percent loss. As an example, should the

## Create Wealth By Preserving Capital

Russell 2000 fall 25 percent and the S&P 500 drop 15 percent from the date of purchase through the maturity date, the note would be up 25 percent. This almost sounds too good to be true.

There is a downside to these notes, however. Should the worst performing index be down more than 30 percent, then the equity-linked note would be down the same percentage as the index. For instance, if the Russell 2000 fell 35 percent, and the S&P 500 were down 25 percent, then the note would lose 35 percent. These notes are designed to be held to maturity, and therefore there are also some liquidity issues. As such these notes should only be utilized for investments with at least a three-year time horizon. Another shortcoming is that the notes are backed by the strength of the bank that issues them. Beware of the next Lehman Brothers or Bear Stearns.

Even considering their limitations, equity-linked notes can be utilized within an overall allocation to potentially dampen downside exposure, especially after a bull market has become long in the tooth. Let's imagine that portfolio A is allocated 100 percent to equities and portfolio B is allocated 70 percent to equities and 30 percent to the above-referenced equity-linked note. To make the example simple, let's say that both indexes will perform the same during the three-year period.

Portfolio B is now long 70 percent equities, with a 30 percent allocation to the equity-barrier note. Should equity markets rise over the three-year period, then portfolios A and B would basically perform the same. However, if equity markets fell 25 percent over the period, there would be a significant difference in performance between the two portfolios. Portfolio A would drop 25 percent, and portfolio B would only lose 10 percent.

If the markets were to fall more than 30 percent, the two portfolios would once again basically perform the same. No harm, no foul.

The intention of this book is to outline the tools that investors have at their fingertips to create wealth by preserving capital. We hope you have enjoyed it.

# Bibliography

Sagi, Jacob S. & Seasholes, Mark S. "Firm-specific attributes & the cross-section of momentum." *Journal of Financial Economics* 48-49 (2005).

# Author Bio

MARK EICKER IS an experienced portfolio manager who has been recognized by the industry for his contributions in the field. He is a managing partner for Sterling Global Strategies, an investment advisory firm in Carlsbad, California.

Eicker is frequently invited to speak at industry events and conferences. He contributes to Forbes and has been quoted in Investor's Business Daily, The Financial Times, ETF.com, and other financial publications.

Eicker and his wife, Rozlyn, reside in Vista, California, and enjoy hiking, traveling, brewing, and reading.

www.ingramcontent.com/pod-product-compliance
Lightning Source LLC
Chambersburg PA
CBHW060404190526
45169CB00002B/749